# The Seeds That Grew and Grew

Matthew 13:1–9; 18–23
for Children

Written by Jeffrey E. Burkart
Illustrated by Chris Sharp

CONCORDIA PUBLISHING HOUSE · SAINT LOUIS

By a lake our Lord sat down,
And soon a large crowd gathered 'round.
So Jesus thought it best to float
Upon the lake inside a boat.

And when He'd climbed aboard He told
The story that will now unfold.
So listen carefully today
And hear what Jesus had to say.

"One day," He said, "a farmer strode
Into his field on which he sowed
Some seeds, in high hopes that they'd grow.
He scattered his seeds to and fro.

"Now, some seed fell upon good ground,
But many seeds that fell were found
Upon a path where birds soon came
And ate the seeds! Now, what a shame.

"On shallow, stony soil some fell.
But those seeds did not do so well.
The hot sun scorched them, and they dried.
They had no roots, and they all died.

"Still other seeds in thorns were sown.
And you could almost hear them groan
Because those seeds were overrun
By thorns that choked each and ev'ry one.

"Those seeds that on the rocks were sown
And those that fell upon the road
And those that tried to quickly grow
Among the thorns were doomed, you know.

"But what about the seeds that found
Their way upon the better ground?
Their story ends quite happily,
As each of you is soon to see.

"The seeds that fell upon good soil
Grew grain that simply could not spoil.
They multiplied a hundredfold,
Which was a great sight to behold."

The people said, "That story's keen,
But tell us, please, what does it mean?"
Then Jesus said, "Now lend an ear.
I will make this story clear.

"The Word of God is like the seed
That's scattered to a world in need.
But some who hear God's Word don't know
What it means, so faith doesn't grow.

"And some who hear God's Word are glad.
They shout for joy, and they're not sad.
But when some trouble comes their way,
They have no roots and fall away.

Bah...

"And there are those who hear God's Word
But care for money—how absurd!
For earthly riches choke the mind;
That person's faith no one can find.

"But when God's Word lands on good earth,
His Holy Spirit will give birth
To faith that grows a hundredfold—
To faith that is both strong and bold."

And God has made us like the earth
Where seeds of faith grow and give birth
To fruits of faith that we can share
With all God's people everywhere.

Dear Parents:

Have your child help you plant some seeds outside or in a flower pot. As you care for the plants and watch them grow, remind your child that God's Word is like seed. When we read God's Word and study it in church and Sunday School, the Holy Spirit helps the faith worked in us at our Baptism to grow.

Plan some ways that you and your child can help sow the seed of God's Word—share this book with a neighbor, send a card with a Christian message to a friend who needs to know Jesus, invite a child to attend Sunday School and church with you. Thank God for nurturing faith in you and your child.

The Editor